MY BATTLE
WITH CHRONIC
FATIGUE SYNDROME

My Battle
with Chronic
Fatigue Syndrome

BECKIE BUTCHER

iUniverse, Inc.
Bloomington

My Battle with Chronic Fatigue Syndrome

iUniverse books may be ordered through booksellers or by contacting:

iUniverse
1663 Liberty Drive
Bloomington, IN 47403
www.iuniverse.com
1-800-Authors (1-800-288-4677)

ISBN: 978-1-4697-7378-0 (sc)
ISBN: 978-1-4697-7379-7 (ebk)

Printed in the United States of America

iUniverse rev. date: 03/08/2012

CONTENTS

Note: this book is based on my experience with Chronic Fatigue Syndrome and mine only. In no way am I speaking for anybody else.

My true emotions are in my writing, and are in no way meant to be offensive.

They're just that, my own feelings and my own emotions based on my own experience.

ACKNOWLEDGEMENTS

To my many wonderful friends who have stuck with me through the good times and the bad times. I don't know where I would be today without your love and support.

To CTA, Inc. Publishing Company for their permission to use inspirational material from the book, "Facing Illness with Hope: Leaning on Jesus," by Reverend Tim Wesemann. Copyright © 2009 by CTA, Inc. Publishing Company. All rights to Reverend Wesemanns' book are reserved to CTA, Inc.

To Deb Jenson for sharing her gift of editing.

To Teresa Speranza, for helping me stay focused and positive.

To Darla Canney, for putting a smile on my face even on my darkest days.

To my minister, Pastor John Nelson for his compassion and his listening ear and to his wife, Pastor Martha Nelson who saved my spiritual life. God Bless you both and thank you for all you've done.

To the CFIDS Association of America, for all of their good work.

To Jody Jaynes, who referred me to Dr. Kyrie Kleinfelter, my healing salvation.

To Dr. Kyrie Kleinfelter, who has helped me tremendously with her gift of healing. I would also like to thank her for her love and support throughout my darkest times.

To Laura Dion Jones and her staff for letting me spread the word and educate the public through her radio show.

Last but not least, to you Mom. Thank you for not leaving my side, even when I was at my darkest and my worst. You'll never know what you mean to me.

Introduction

My name is Beckie Butcher. I was born and raised in Elgin, Illinois and attended Elgin High School, graduating in 1982. In 1997, I graduated from Elgin Community College with an Associate of Applied Science Degree in Medical Laboratory Technology. In 2007, I was stricken with a debilitating autoimmune disease (a disease in which your immune system attacks your own body) known as Chronic Fatigue Syndrome or CFS. The exact cause of CFS is not known, but it is suspected that certain viruses are the culprits. One such virus is The Epstein-Barr virus, a herpes virus which causes infectious mononucleosis. According to an article in Science Daily (October 2, 2008) research has shown the virus is linked to certain kinds of cancer.

This book is about my experience with the disease and the challenges which it presents. I am sharing my story because I want to reach out and help those who struggle with this as well as those who love and care for them. I want to offer hope to those who are suffering because the truth is, there is hope. Hope springs eternal and we should never give up on it. My wish for you is to find comfort in knowing you are not alone.

There is something else which needs to be said; this is not all in our heads. Chronic Fatigue Syndrome patients truly suffer. It is a serious illness which attacks the organs, muscles, and nervous system. We are not simply "tired." We do not need a good night's sleep or more vitamins. It's much more than that. All the sleep in the world does not help. It is not a refreshing sleep. If it were that simple none of us would be having problems. Many patients are bedridden for years with this; some patients have to crawl to get anywhere. Some patients don't have the strength to stand up. I had to hang on the wall to walk when I first became ill. This is real, and we need help. Our voices need to be heard, and I am proud to be one of those voices.

My Life Before Chronic Fatigue Syndrome

Before I became ill, my interests were church, cooking and entertaining friends. I sang in the choir and taught Sunday school and from 1986 to 2007 I worked in various clinical laboratories. In 2007, I left the laboratory to pursue a career in culinary arts, as cooking had been a lifelong passion of mine. That May I enrolled in Elgin Community Colleges' Culinary Arts Program with dreams of opening my own catering service with a menu of reasonably priced homemade meals appropriately named The Butcher's Block. In July of that same year, I saw my hopes start to fade.

Things were suddenly" foggy." I literally saw fog in front of my face. I became confused; I would ask the same questions over and over again in class. People became very annoyed with me. It was all I could do just to get up in the morning. Every joint and muscle in my body ached. I remember walking down to the kitchen one afternoon having no idea whatsoever who I was or where I was. After almost twenty years of living alone, I was afraid to live alone. Eventually, I couldn't get out of bed except to eat and use the washroom. That alone took all the strength I had. I couldn't hold a simple conversation. But there was nothing clinically wrong with me. My physical examinations were fine. My lab work was fine. For all practical purposes I was fine. But I wasn't; I was terrified. The irony of it was after twenty years of helping others, I was helpless to myself. There I was with all this knowledge and I didn't know what to do with any of it. I knew too much but didn't know anything. In 2007, at the age of 43, I thought I was going to die.

THE MOMENT OF TRUTH: THE DIAGNOSIS

It was August 22nd, 2007, I remember it well. I was sitting in a room at my doctor's office waiting for the results of my lab work. He walks in, shakes my hand, and tells me my Epstein-Barr Early Antigen is high . . . . very high. It was twenty times what it should have been. Then the bomb dropped. He told me I had chronic fatigue syndrome. I was devastated. My jaw dropped and I felt my eyes get bigger and bigger. My heart just sank. I was sick to my stomach and my heart was beating a mile a minute. I could hardly speak. I couldn't believe it. I was then referred to an infectious disease specialist.

After the initial shock wore off I decided the first thing I was going to do was find a support group to help me through this. I felt tough and ready to fight this with everything I had. I told my mother and I told a couple of my friends I was bigger than this, and I wasn't going to let it get the best of me.

Denial perhaps? I think so. I just wasn't aware of it at the time.

So I found an online support group that very night called dailystrength.org. I wasn't going to waste any time in my war against this disease. I met many wonderful friends there who loved, supported and encouraged me. I got a lot out of reading about other people's experiences and I was given a lot of good advice. I was also warned; the person I least expected to turn and walk away from me would turn and walk away from me. Well, that person did just that, and it tore me up for several years. I was devastated by it. It was worse than a death for me because it wasn't a death at all. It was a conscious decision made of this person's own free will.

A death is not a choice, but a conscious decision is, and this near and dear person's conscious decision to walk away from me rather than stick by me in my darkest hour hurt me to the core. In the meantime, life went on as it should and I decided I would live my life as I was able and I would rest when I needed to rest. My doctors told me to do the same. However, those "rests" would last four to six weeks. Still, I had never been one to sit home and feel sorry for myself and I wasn't about to start. I had help physically. My mother is close by, and when I needed food or laundry or anything else she did for me. I tried to always remember there were people worse off than I. At least I wasn't dying. I would get better; it was just a matter of time. I would tell myself over and over this virus would go away eventually. It would just take time. Maybe months maybe years, but it will go away. I was ok with that . . . . for awhile.

While I was doing" ok," I came to the realization I would have to swallow some pride. I realized I wasn't the only one who needed help. Mom did too. It was hard to do, but I eventually decided to let my church help me out by bringing me meals. I had done for others in that way and I decided maybe it was my turn to be taken care of. So I swallowed my pride and asked for help. It was comforting to know people were willing to help that way, but at the same time I had to admit loss of independence. I had always been a hard working, self-sufficient, self-supporting independent woman who was used to doing everything for myself. It was a tough pill to swallow. But I continued to reach out to others through church as I was able because it helped me stop thinking about my own problems. Focusing on others less fortunate than I made me forget, at least for awhile. But still, things were different. I wasn't like everybody else anymore. I was different; I was disabled. I knew this, but I didn't realize it. I was still" ok," or was I?

HOPE FOR THE FUTURE

When my church was helping me out with meals, one of the ladies told me of a chiropractor who treated people with chronic fatigue syndrome and fibromyalgia. Her treatments really helped these patients. It is called the NUCCA method (National Upper Cervical Chiropractic Association). It works like this; at the base of the skull there are two small bones called the axis and the atlas. They are the first two vertebrae of the spinal cord. When the atlas, also known as cervical vertebra 1 or C-1 is out of alignment, the cranial nerves, the nerves from the brain which send messages to the body, are pinched and these messages are unable to reach the body. This being the case, the body is unable to function as it should, causing problems such as headache, neck and shoulder pain as well

7

as muscle and joint pain. After the atlas has been adjusted and put back into alignment however, the messages are able to get through and the body can begin to heal itself. The time it takes the body to completely heal varies from person to person, and it takes the body approximately one month to heal every year of damage. Since I was 43 when I started treatment, it will take me approximately three and a half to four years to heal, which I have found to be true. I have been getting treatment now for two and a half years, and I feel much better. I am not completely well yet, but I feel I am well on my way. I have included images in the back of the book as points of reference. For more information on the NUCCA method, visit nucca. org.

In the meantime, I started to feel better and started looking for work. I got a good paying job which was close to home with people I enjoyed working with. I couldn't have been happier. I was moving forward and was looking into getting my Bachelor's Degree in Chemistry. All went well for the first week or so. Then I became exhausted again. I wasn't just tired from working. I couldn't keep up. I lost that job after three weeks because I was seriously ill all over again. There I was, home, sick on the couch, barely able to move from systemic pain and extreme exhaustion. I was home more than I was there.

On my last day, I went home ten minutes after I got there. I told my boss I didn't want to lose my job, but I knew it was coming. I could hardly stand up. On the way home that day, I realized I was truly disabled. I had to admit I was still very ill. This meant I had to face my demons, and I wasn't ready to do that. I cried and cried, and I asked my maker, now what? What was I supposed to do now? Where was I supposed to go from here? What did He want from me? I had to face my disease and everything it meant for me; the inability to work and stand on my own two feet. I had to face the fact my life had been taken away from me even though I wasn't dying. My life as I knew it was over, and I had to face the fact I wasn't "ok" as I mentioned earlier. I tried and I failed.

Later that week, I made an appointment to counsel with my minister. Once again, I cried my eyes out. I asked him, why? What had I done to deserve this? I didn't understand why this happened to me when all my life I tried to be a good person. I didn't even apply for social security disability right away because I thought maybe I would recover within six months to a year and I wouldn't have to use that. But I was wrong. He said I didn't do anything. It just happened and now I have to decide what I was going to do with it. I had to find a way to make the best of it in my life. I had no idea what I was going to do with it. When I left church I had a lot to digest and sort out. We had discussed the five stages of grief, and after talking with him, I realized I was somewhere between anger and acceptance. I couldn't deny it anymore, so I became angry, very angry. I was angry about having to live in a body that wouldn't let me live normally. There for awhile I lived in a body that would only let me exist. There was anger towards people who told me they were sure it was a thyroid problem and all I needed was a pill and I would be fine. They then proceeded to make my situation all about them and didn't listen to me at all. Like a doctor isn't going to think of that? That's one of the first things they look for as well as adrenal insufficiency. People belittled the seriousness of my illness as if they didn't believe me. They meant well, but had no idea how cruel they were truly being. I was angry at people who said they think they may have chronic fatigue syndrome also because they're tired all the time too. As I said earlier, it's not about being tired. It is a serious and debilitating disease which attacks the body's own tissues.

I continued to help others as I had always done because I didn't think sitting home and feeling sorry for myself would make it go away, which, it doesn't. What I didn't realize however, was I had to take time for myself and work through this and start to heal emotionally, and I refused to do that. I didn't take time to grieve my disease, because it meant having to give into it and admit it was real. I didn't want to do that either. Although it wasn't fatal and I wasn't going to die, I still lost my life. As a result of not putting myself first and not taking the "me" time I needed, I became a dark, horrible, and ugly person who wasn't good for anything or anybody. I knew for months I couldn't go on like that, but I just could not grieve and let my emotions out. The tears just wouldn't come. I felt nothing. I was numb. I think I was so enveloped in anger there was nothing else. I knew this was self-destructive and one day I would explode. Well, one day I did. I was at my mom's house. Three years of anger, frustration, crying and screaming came out. Cursing and flying objects were involved; it wasn't pretty. My poor dear mother just stood there numb. She didn't know what to do or say. I was violent and out of control. I'd had enough; enough of being compliant and complacent and all smiles and saying it was ok. No, it is NOT ok! It's a terrible disease, one I wouldn't wish on anybody. I was at my lowest and my worst that day. My life had no purpose. I felt useless. I tried to better myself by trying to take classes, but I couldn't even do that. It took way too much out of me. I was in bed for weeks afterwards. I wished I could die. At least it would end then. My mother's worrying about me and her financial worries would end. I truly thought she would be better off without me.

Things were better for awhile after that day. Then I suffered another severe flare up. I wished I could have died all over again. No, I wanted to die. Once again I felt my life had no purpose and once again, I thought my mother would be better off if I was no longer here for her to have to take care of and worry about.

THE DAY MY LIFE CHANGED

The date was June 27th, 2010. The place was Hosanna! Lutheran Church, St. Charles, Illinois. The time, eleven o'clock A.M. My minister was out of town that weekend with his children. Since his wife Martha is also a minister, he asked her to speak that day. Am I glad he did. The preaching series was on GPS and her sermon was about how God allowed u-turns in our lives. This really hit home with me, because I seriously needed a u-turn. I was starting to get away from God; the way I lived, what I said, how I thought was not Godlike at all. He really should have been ashamed of me as His Child, but I was at the point where I didn't care anymore. I saw no evidence of Him in my life. I was seriously ill, someone very near and dear to me had deserted me in my darkest hour and people who I thought cared about me weren't very nice to me, what was there to believe in? I hated everybody, including myself. There were occasions, however when I would see little booklets at church and I would pick them up and start reading them. I guess I wasn't too far gone. I did turn to spiritual, uplifting material to help myself.

This statement changed my life. "All circumstances, no matter how bad, God will make them good." Wow! What a wake up call. This feeling of peace just washed over me like a tidal wave. It was a cleansing feeling. It was that day I realized no matter how bad things got, I was going to be ok, because The Lord was there to help me through whatever was ahead.

She then went on to say how when we stray from Him, He is not mad at us, but rather He is concerned about us, and we can get back into relationship with Him. He calls us back to Him and we can get back into His ways. But we must first admit we failed; God is not surprised at this. He waits for us to admit our failures. He then invites us to accept Him; however, we must first accept His forgiveness. He WANTS to forgive us. Once we do, the distance between us and God shortens. He will not remove the consequences of our actions, but He will fix it and cleanse our relationship because He is always there for us. He has great love for us. Lastly, we must ask for revised directions. He will give them to us and tell us where He wants us to be; He will meet us there. We must act quickly on His instructions to do our part in the relationship. God does not give up on us, rather he empowers us and gives us the energy to do His Will, once we ask for and accept His revised directions. We are to study His Word and remember it is not OUR WILL be done but THY WILL be done.

I had a lot thrown at me in sixty minutes. I had a lot to think about and digest. And not just that day either. The next day I went out and bought highlighting pens and the best Bible I could find and I started to read. I just read and read until I found passages which were really helpful to me. Romans 5:3-5 is one of them. The passage reads:

> "Not only so, but we also rejoice in our sufferings, because we know that suffering produces perseverance; perseverance, character; and character, hope. And hope does not disappoint us, because God has poured out his love into our hearts by the Holy Spirit, whom he has given us."

15

I have found this to be true. I have grown in many ways since this happened to me. I have grown in understanding, tolerance, and faith. It is easy to believe when things are easy. When things are easy there is no challenge, no test of faith. I know many people who have always had it good and who have never known problems. They are happy, but I have also noticed simplicity in them. Not that they are simple as in shallow, but they just don't know or understand anything else but an easy, simple life. They have never been challenged. It's not their fault, however, I have felt many times like they don't even want to understand or care. I have felt like certain people would rather avoid the whole thing and not get their hands dirty with something that's difficult to understand. I have often wondered what would happen if something truly devastating happened to them. Would their faith be shaken? I must admit, mine was for awhile. I had heard all those words before, and it was easy for me to believe, too. But when devastation became a reality for me, I wasn't so sure. Not after awhile, anyway. It was a lot easier not to believe. It was a lot safer. But I kept going to church, so I knew I must not have strayed too far from God. He always found me, whether I wanted Him to or not. He still does.

Another point which is clear to me in this passage is hope does not disappoint us. With God there IS hope, and hope doesn't leave us. Even certain family members weren't always very nice to me. But God will never do that to us. He is always there, listening and loving. As angry and frustrated as I still get at times, it's always followed by peace. I get this calming feeling, and once again I know that everything will be all right. God is in control. It is because of Him I wake up every morning, able to face a new day and make it through that day, no matter what I have thrown at me. I'm still alive at the end of the day.

In Proverbs, chapter 2:1-8 it says this:

> "My son, if you accept my words and store up my commandments within you, turning your ear to wisdom and applying your heart to understanding, and if you call out for insight and cry aloud for understanding, and if you look for it as for silver and search for it as for hidden treasure, then you will understand the fear of the Lord and find the knowledge of God. For the Lord gives wisdom, and from his mouth come knowledge and understanding. He holds victory in store for the upright, he is a shield to those whose walk is blameless, for

17

> he guards the course of the just and protects
> the way of his faithful ones."

Interesting words. I had done this many times without realizing it. I would cry bitter tears and call out," Why, why!" to my maker. Why did this happen to me? What had I done to deserve this? What had I done that I had to suffer so in more ways than one? If faith could move mountains why wouldn't He heal me? Why was He allowing this? Was He really a good and loving God?

I wanted answers. I wanted and needed to understand. I was calling out and seeking. Then that peaceful feeling would come to me. I could never put into words what it meant; I just knew everything would be all right. I would be taken care of one way or another. I was able to trust Him.

Another thing I finally was able to understand was I was indeed, blameless. I had done nothing to deserve this. It was something that just happened. Am I happy about it? No, of course I'm not, but as my minister pointed out to me it's the hand I was dealt and it was up to me what I did with it. Was I going to feel sorry for myself or was I going to turn it around into something positive? Although I have to admit, there were times I felt sorry for myself, too. It is through the bad that I am able to write this book. I am sharing my trials and tribulations with you with the hope that I may help you and give you some comfort and understanding of this devastating disease. I want to offer you hope and give you the strength to deal with your circumstance and reach out to others as I have reached out to you. This is the good that can come out of the bad. This is what can happen when you stay faithful to God.

Proverbs chapter 3:5-6 says:

> "Trust in the Lord with all your heart and lean not on your own understanding; in all your ways acknowledge him, and he will make your paths straight."

Trust Him. Only He knows the answers, and they are the right answers. Only He can make your life right.

Proverbs 4:23 offers this advice to us:

> "Above all else, guard your heart, for it is the wellspring of life."

Keep your heart open to God and all others. Keep it open so you may show others the kindness and compassion you would like to be shown you in your time of trouble.

Isaiah 40: 28-31 gives us comfort in these words:

> "Do you not know? Have you not heard? The Lord is the everlasting God, the Creator of the ends of the earth. He will not grow tired or weary, and his understanding no one can fathom. He gives strength to the weary and increases the power of the weak. Even youths grow tired and weary, and young men stumble and fall; but those who hope in the Lord will renew their strength. They will soar on wings like eagles; they will run and not grow weary, they will walk and not be faint."

We make it to the end of the day because He walks by our side, giving us the strength we need.

Hope For The Future Through God And Through Jesus.

One day while at church I noticed a small booklet entitled," Facing Illness With Hope: Leaning On Jesus," by Reverend Tim Wesemann. It explains how Jesus understands what we are going through because of how He suffered to the extreme and how we were on His mind and in His heart while He suffered. He goes on to explain how because of His life, death and resurrection, the pain and sickness in the world will one day die.

Also, God knows our bodies better than anybody; better than we do and better than our doctors do because He

21

created it. The world we live in is broken by sin and it has invaded our bodies, however, Gods' promise to us is to work for our good through what we're facing right now. Reverend Wessemann says to us there is hope. Even though our lives and the lives of our loved ones have been interrupted, there is still hope. Although things look and feel bad, we are not crushed, destroyed, or abandoned. Jesus is there, walking us through our every difficulty.

He gives us five questions to ask God and our friends and family.

Five questions to ask God.

1) Why?
2) How will you reveal yourself to me? In big ways or small ways?
3) Will you give me grace sufficient to accept things I cannot understand? Will you give me grace to trust in your promise to use every circumstance for your glory?
4) Will you open doors for me which will allow me to share my faith in Jesus Christ with others so they will come to know the hope offered by Him?
5) Will you strengthen my faith so I will hold firmly to the hope you provide in Jesus daily?

Five questions to ask family and friends.

1) Will you remind me of the hope I have through the promises and presence of Jesus Christ whether I'm having good days or bad days?

2) Will you make sure I stay as concerned about my spiritual health as I am about my physical health?

3) Will you find it in your heart to forgive me if and when my personal struggles interfere with our relationship?

4) Will you respect the fact we may deal with hardships in different as well as unexpected ways, all the while praying our lives will glorify God?

5) Will you pray with me as well as for me?

God IS there for you. He's the reason you wake up every morning. He's the reason you're still here.

SOME FINAL THOUGHTS

I call this the anger chapter of my book, because of things well-meaning people said that were in reality, hurtful, and as a result I was very angry with them. I also call it the anger chapter because here is where I say things that might make people angry; however, these are things that need to be said. Here are some examples:

1) There are people in a lot worse situations than you. People love to say this. Although they mean well, they really don't know what they are saying or how that sounds. How could they possibly know that? Have they walked in those other people's shoes or mine? No, they have not. What's more is they don't even know those "other" people, so how can they possibly

make that kind of comparison? What gives them the right? If I sound angry here it's because I am. Why? Because there is nothing meaner than belittling something you don't understand rather than taking the time to care about another human being as far as I'm concerned. It's happened to me more times than I care to count. Chronic Fatigue Syndrome is serious. Also, it's been my experience it's people who have never struggled with illness a day in their lives who say this. I spent three months in bed scared to death I was dying. Until one has experienced this kind of uncertainty and fear for their lives, they have no business talking to ANYBODY like that. It's not about other people; it's about the person who is scared and struggling at that particular time. Could it have been worse? Sure, but things could have been better too. What's more is I didn't need people devaluing what it was because what I was going through was very real and very scary. I needed to be validated in my own situation, not compared to other people. I couldn't think about others at that point. Not that I felt sorry for myself, I didn't. At least not much; that's not me. But I was scared and I needed my friends to listen to me, not cut me off and belittle the situation. That's never a good thing to do. I'd like my audience to take a moment and say that out loud. Listen to how it sounds, then put the shoe on the other foot.

2) People with problems need to stop all the drama and drop the "look at me" attitude and reach out to each other. Drama? Excuse me? Since when is feeling the need to talk to someone and be listened to being dramatic? Unless of course I had gone on and on about it and taken the "poor little me" attitude, which I did not. I resented the insinuation from this person that I do. When people ask me about it, I explain it to them and that's it. I don't like to talk about it much. Why? What for? Dwelling on it isn't going to make it go away any faster. When I'm in the company of others, I like to forget about it for awhile and be happy, not bring everybody else down. Not only is this a mean thing to say, but it is also hurtful and ignorant, and it's been my experience that people who say this don't want to deal with it or me. Fine, don't ask me about it then. I agree people need to reach out and help each other; HOWEVER . . . . it is not about drama and a "look at me" attitude.

Serious illness has some devastating effects, physically, mentally, and emotionally. I needed to be listened to and understood. As for the "look at me" attitude, again, people need to be validated according to their own situation. Not every illness is the same, neither is every person. We're human beings, not robots, and we all cope with and react differently to illness. People do not need to be criticized and judged by someone who has never walked in their shoes. I felt like I was being told to shut up and deal with it. Well, I've been dealing with it for a long time, and let me tell you, it gets very old, very fast.

3) Just because we're a bunch of idiots doesn't mean we don't understand. Nobody can do everything right all of the time. What? Where did that come from? It's not about doing things right all of the time. I'm just saying listen, don't judge, and just be there if and when I need you, that's all. I have no idea what this person was thinking when this was said. Wherever it came from, I didn't need the sarcasm. I was also laughed at by this person because I said I could never tolerate a three hour car ride. I still can't, not yet. Laughing at a seriously ill person is as low as it gets. Glad this person thought it was so funny. This is just one example of how cruel some people can be.

I'm not saying be selfish and self-absorbed here. I would never say that. People do need to reach out to others, but there are times when you have to focus and take care of yourself. Why do you think I wrote this book? Why do you think I've been on live local radio speaking out about this? For the same reason I want to do research for Chronic Fatigue Syndrome when I'm well. I want to reach out to others and give them hope and give something back to the others who struggle with this awful disease.

4) Chiropractors won't do you any good; they just want your money. First of all, and I am in no way lessening the value of other chiropractic methods here, but the NUCCA method is the only thing that has helped me. No other doctor has. I was given an antiviral medication to no avail. I was then given an anti-depressant because one of the side-effects can make people more energetic. I was more energetic all right. My heart raced, I shook like a leaf and I had seizures. Second of all, this is just an opinion and while everyone is entitled to their opinion, this is one instance when it can be detrimental. If anyone would take what these people say to heart, they could miss out on being healed and getting their lives back. Besides, it's a matter of hope . . . . I did not need these people to take my hope away . . . . hope was all I had at that point. I needed their support and encouragement. And if it had been bogus I'd have found out sooner or later anyway.

One point of reference I would like to share is a wonderful video brought to us by the CFIDS Association of America entitled, "What Would You Do." It's a four minute video on Youtube.com. Approximately 1700 people were asked what they would do if they were well. Some of the answers are surprising because they are the little things in life which most of us take for granted. It's truly heartbreaking to watch. It gets the point across as to how serious Chronic Fatigue Syndrome really is. It's nothing to mess with or belittle. It's out there and people need help. If you would like to learn more about Chronic Fatigue syndrome, watch this video. To learn more about research for it, visit cfids.org. Both of these resources are very informative.

Another bit of information I would like to share is the issue of gluten. Gluten is a protein found in not all, but many grains, including wheat, malt, and barley. It is also found in many food additives and is hard to stay away from. It doesn't affect everybody like this, but it causes severe autoimmune flare-ups in me. My joints and muscles ache and I get as stiff as a board. I wind up in bed if I eat too much of it. For a list of safe and unsafe foods, visit celiac.com.

CONCLUSION

These last things are what have helped me in my battle.

1) Let go of past hurts and anger. Negative emotions are stresses on the body, and stress does not help the healing process. Two things which have helped me immensely are meditation and yoga. What I do is meditate first thing in the morning when I wake up before all those "voices" start nagging at me, reminding me of all my daily stresses and worries. Lying down is fine, as long as you are comfortable. Pay close attention to the rise and fall of your chest as you breathe. Check your mind. Clear it. This is not an easy thing to do, so if it helps, focus on a picture, smell or prayer. I focus on water; the ocean,

a lake, a waterfall, or a beach. Water is very soothing to me. It takes practice to control your mind, so don't give up if you're not successful after the first few times. Stick with it. It's amazing how much more relaxed you'll feel once you're learned to control your mind and not let it control you. I am able to handle daily stresses much more effectively, I'm not nearly as short-tempered as I used to be, and my muscles are not nearly as tense. Meditating before bed makes me forget what happened during the day and I sleep much better. Twenty minutes of deep meditation is the equivalent of three hours of sleep.

2) Stop fighting so hard. Once I was able to stop fighting and saying I will not let this get in my way, I started to feel better and heal faster. It happened, yes, it stinks, yes, but it's nothing you can change. Accept it as a part of you life, at least for now.

3) Get help. See a NUCCA chiropractor and have yourself evaluated. You have nothing to lose if you can be helped. It won't happen overnight, but it will happen, and it will have been worth the wait.

4) Pray. Ask The Lord's help in your struggle. He created you; therefore He will give you what you need. He knows you better than anybody.

5) Journal. It is very important to get your feelings out. They will fester within otherwise, and once again,

there will be negative stress eating at your body. One thing I have done is go back to previous entries from months before, and I can see how far I have come.

6) Eat a healthy diet, exercise as you can tolerate and take your vitamins. Everybody should do that anyway.

7) Surround yourself with positive, happy people and stay away from those who bring you down. Happiness is an essential part of healing; at least it has been for me. Keep your chin up, think happy thoughts, make the best of it for now~ and don't let ANYBODY tell you how you feel. There is good that can come out of the bad. For me it was writing this book and speaking out about this on a local radio show. You need to figure out what it is for you. And please do. That is healing also. A kind of catharsis if you will.

Finally, to all of you who struggle or watch someone who struggles, I hope this helps. If I have reached one person through this book, I will have done what I set out to do. My love to you all and I wish you the best.

In memory of my father, Richard James Butcher
who gave me so much.

June 15, 1930-May 24th, 1985

Presentiment is that long shadow

On the lawn,

Indicative that suns go down;

The notice to the startled grass

That darkness is about to pass.

Emily Dickenson.

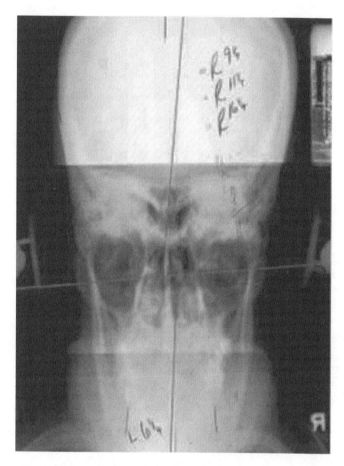

If you look at the lines drawn here (pre correction) you can
see the misalignment of the atlas or C-1. When the neck is
like this, the body is out of balance and the messages from
the brain are unable to reach the body. This is what causes
headaches and systemic discomfort.

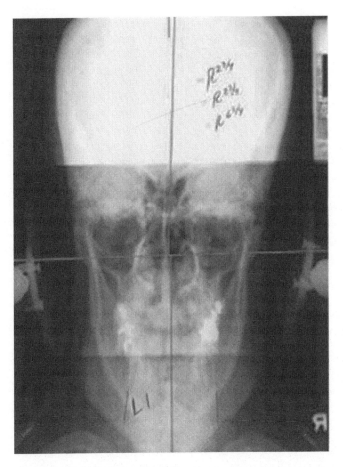

If you look at the lines drawn here (post correction) you can see C-1 is back in alignment and the body is able to function and heal as it should.